THE ANIMAL FILES
WE NEED
SHARKS

by Lisa Bullard

FOCUS
READERS

WWW.FOCUSREADERS.COM

Focus Readers is distributed by North Star Editions:
sales@northstareditions.com | 888-417-0195

Produced for Focus Readers by Red Line Editorial.

Content Consultant: Stephen M. Kajiura, Professor of Biological Sciences, Florida Atlantic University

Photographs ©: lindsay_imagery/iStockphoto, cover, 1; USO/iStockphoto, 4–5; Lebendkulturen.de/Shutterstock Images, 7 (phytoplankton); British Antarctic Survey/ Science Source, 7 (krill); Mansiliya Yury/Shutterstock Images, 7 (fish); Leonardo Gonzalez/ Shutterstock Images, 7 (sea lion); 3DMI/Shutterstock Images, 7 (shark); Scubazoo/Science Source, 9; Milkov Vladislav/Shutterstock Images, 10–11; Laura Dinraths/Shutterstock Images, 13; stephan kerkhofs/Shutterstock Images, 15; Below_Surface/iStockphoto, 16–17; Lano Lan/Shutterstock Images, 19; Suwarin Rachanikorn/Shutterstock Images, 21; Louise Murray/robertharding/Newscom, 23; shells1/iStockphoto, 24–25; dikobraziy/Shutterstock Images, 27; Jeffrey Rotman/Science Source, 29

Library of Congress Cataloging-in-Publication Data
Names: Bullard, Lisa, author.
Title: We need sharks / by Lisa Bullard.
Description: Lake Elmo, MN : Focus Readers, [2019] | Series: The animal files
   | Audience: Grade 4 to 6. | Includes index.
Identifiers: LCCN 2018026612 (print) | LCCN 2018027293 (ebook) | ISBN
   9781641854887 (PDF) | ISBN 9781641854306 (ebook) | ISBN 9781641853149
   (hardcover : alk. paper) | ISBN 9781641853729 (paperback : alk. paper)
Subjects: LCSH: Sharks--Ecology--Juvenile literature.
Classification: LCC QL638.9 (ebook) | LCC QL638.9 .B824 2019 (print) | DDC
   597.3/4--dc23
LC record available at https://lccn.loc.gov/2018026612

Printed in the United States of America
Mankato, MN
October, 2018

ABOUT THE AUTHOR

Lisa Bullard is the author of more than 90 books for children, including the mystery novel *Turn Left at the Cow*. She also teaches writing classes for adults and children. Lisa grew up in Minnesota and now lives just north of Minneapolis.

TABLE OF CONTENTS

CHAPTER 1

The Great Hunter 5

CHAPTER 2

A Predator People Need 11

CHAPTER 3

Sharks at Risk 17

THAT'S AMAZING!

Diving with Sharks 22

CHAPTER 4

Saving Sharks 25

Focus on Sharks • 30
Glossary • 31
To Learn More • 32
Index • 32

THE GREAT HUNTER

One of the world's mightiest **predators** is on the move. It tracks its **prey** through ocean waters. The shark has strong hunting skills. This large fish smells, hears, and senses its prey in the water. The shark closes in. It strikes! Rows of sharp teeth rip into a sea lion.

A great white shark jumps out of the water with its prey.

There are more than 500 **species** of sharks. Different species eat different types of prey. Several shark species are top predators. This means other animals do not hunt them.

Sharks play an important role in many ocean **food chains**. One example of a food chain starts with single-celled life-forms. These life-forms are eaten by shrimp-like animals called krill. The krill are then eaten by small fish. And the small fish are eaten by sea lions. The sea lions, in turn, become shark prey.

Ecosystems have many different food chains. Together, the food chains in an ecosystem form a food web. Sharks are at the top of many ocean food webs. They help ocean ecosystems stay in balance.

FISH FOOD

A food chain of the great white shark

phytoplankton
(single-celled life-forms)

krill

small fish

great white shark

sea lion

Without sharks, the species they prey on would increase. And if that happened, all those extra animals would need food. Species that are lower on the food chain would be eaten in higher numbers. They might even die out.

DO SHARKS HUNT PEOPLE?

Movies and TV often show sharks as dangerous killers. But sharks rarely bite humans without cause. If a human tries to grab a shark, the shark will fight back. In 2017, there were only 88 cases of sharks going after humans without a reason. Only five of those cases ended in a person's death. Experts believed these events were accidents. The sharks did not mean to hunt the humans.

A blacktip reef shark feeds on the body of a dead fish.

Sharks keep prey populations healthy. They target sick or injured animals. This allows stronger animals to continue the species. Some sharks eat animals that have already died. They prevent the dead animals from spreading disease.

CHAPTER 2

A PREDATOR PEOPLE NEED

Humans need healthy oceans. Ocean plants create much of the oxygen people breathe. Oceans also help control the weather. They move heat across the planet. Many communities depend on oceans. People ship products across the water. Sea animals and plants also provide humans with food and medicines.

Sharks live in all of Earth's oceans.

Sharks help make these things possible by keeping oceans healthy.

Some people's jobs depend on oceans. Decreasing shark populations can affect these jobs. When ocean ecosystems are in balance, there are plenty of fish to catch. But if shark numbers decrease, other species might decrease as well. This could threaten fishers' jobs.

Humans rely on various parts of ocean ecosystems. One example is seagrass. When seagrass grows long, small fish live inside it. When the fish grow, they become a source of food for humans. Seagrass has other benefits, too. It cleans the water and creates oxygen. It also

Seagrass is home to a variety of animals, including seahorses.

prevents shorelines from wearing away.
Perhaps most importantly, seagrass
stores large amounts of carbon dioxide.
This gas can be harmful for the planet if
too much of it enters Earth's atmosphere.

Seagrass decreases the amount of gas released. This helps protect the planet.

Without sharks, there would be less seagrass. Scientists made this discovery in Shark Bay, Australia. Shark Bay is home to tiger sharks. It is also home to shark prey, including sea turtles and

SHARKS AND HUMAN HEALTH

Sharks may provide clues for keeping humans healthy. For example, one scientist studies the healthy **bacteria** found on sharks' skin. First, she scrapes samples off the skin. Then, she sends the sharks back into the water. Afterward, she studies the samples. She wants to use the bacteria to create new medicines. Humans could take the medicines to treat infections.

A green sea turtle feeds on seagrass.

sea cows. These two animals eat large amounts of seagrass. But in certain areas of Shark Bay, they stay away from the seagrass. They know that sharks swim nearby. In these areas, the seagrass is left to grow. In other locations, sea turtles eat all the seagrass. These spots have fewer sharks to scare the turtles away.

CHAPTER 3

SHARKS AT RISK

Sharks have existed for more than 400 million years. They were on the planet before the dinosaurs. But today, many shark species are at risk. Some examples are great hammerheads, whale sharks, and several kinds of angel sharks.

Humans pose the greatest danger to sharks. **Overfishing** is a common threat.

The great white shark is one of the oldest existing species on Earth.

Shark fishing has increased in the last few decades. Each year, fishers kill more than 100 million sharks.

When fishers catch sharks, they often cut off their fins. This is called finning. It allows fishers to fit more fins on their boats. That way, they can make more money. The fishers return finned sharks

TOO FEW SHARKS

Overfishing is a problem for many types of fish. But it is an especially large threat to sharks. Sharks have babies later in life than many other fish. They also have fewer babies at a time. This means there are fewer sharks to replace the ones that are killed. As a result, the shark population falls.

After finning sharks, fishers let the fins dry in the sun.

to the sea. Without their fins, the sharks can't swim properly. They eventually die.

Many of these fins are used to make shark fin soup. This ancient Chinese dish is popular in several Asian countries.

People often eat it at celebrations. Shark parts are also used in other products. These include certain types of makeup and shoes.

Some fishers catch sharks by accident. These sharks are called bycatch. Fishers catch them while fishing for other animals. Other people fish for sharks for fun. Fishers often return the sharks they catch to the ocean. But in some cases, the sharks are too stressed or injured to survive.

Humans also threaten sharks by building along coastlines. Sometimes, people dig underwater when they build. This can disturb the habitats of young

Millions of sharks are killed each year to make shark fin soup.

sharks. Humans also pollute the ocean. The water can become so unclean that plants and animals cannot live there. When that happens, the food webs that support sharks can fall apart.

DIVING WITH SHARKS

Some people pay to meet sharks face-to-face. Diving with sharks is known as shark **tourism**. Sometimes, divers stay in an underwater cage. This protects them from sharks.

Not everyone believes that shark tourism is a good idea. Tour companies often attract sharks with bait. The bait draws sharks toward the divers. Some people worry that bait will change sharks' behavior. The sharks might start to identify divers with food. Visitors might also harm these locations. For instance, they could damage coral reefs. Or they could pollute the water with trash.

Other people think shark tourism will help save sharks. By seeing sharks, visitors might be more likely to protect them. Shark tourism brings in lots of money. If sharks die out, ocean communities

A great white shark swims by tourists who are shark diving.

will make less money. Therefore, humans have a reason to protect sharks. Because of tourism, sharks are worth more alive than dead.

CHAPTER 4

SAVING SHARKS

If humans do not change their behavior, some sharks could die out. Thankfully, more and more people want to save sharks. People are learning about the importance of the animal. They are also learning about the threats facing sharks. Education is the first step to **conservation**.

People in Sydney, Australia, protest the killing of sharks.

Attitudes about shark fin soup are changing, too. In China, fewer people eat the soup. In 2012, the Chinese government announced it would stop serving the soup at government events. Several countries also have laws against shark finning. Many airlines no longer allow fins on their planes. This makes it harder to send fins around the world.

Other changes are happening as well. The United Nations is a worldwide group that helps countries work together. The group passed laws to manage the trade of some shark species. Many countries have created shark **sanctuaries**. In these areas, shark fishing is limited or not allowed.

Scientists are also studying safe limits for shark fishing. Their goal is to allow fishing in numbers that maintain healthy shark populations.

SAFE SEAS

Shark sanctuaries around the world

Maldives

Palau

Federated States of Micronesia

Marshall Islands

Kiribati

PACIFIC OCEAN

French Polynesia

Samoa

AUSTRALIA

New Caledonia

Cook Islands

INDIAN OCEAN

NORTH AMERICA

The Bahamas

Dominican Republic

Honduras

British Virgin Islands

Sint Maarten

Saba

Cayman Islands

Bonaire

ATLANTIC OCEAN

Some countries that protect sharks are seeing results. For example, scientists in one study counted sharks off the US East Coast. Between 2012 and 2015, sharks increased by 55 percent.

But sharks still face many problems. Shark fin soup remains popular in places, including Thailand and Vietnam. Not all countries have adopted laws to protect sharks. A shark that is protected near one country is still at risk in other waters. And even in places where laws do exist, people do not always follow them.

Another challenge is that scientists do not know enough about sharks. It is hard to count and study animals in the ocean.

Scientists put a tracking tag on a lemon shark in Bimini, Bahamas.

Scientists need more money for research. As they learn more, people will be better able to save sharks.

Shark conservation takes time, money, and hard work. But more and more people believe the effort is worth it. By protecting sharks, humans protect the oceans. And by protecting the oceans, humans can protect all life on Earth.

FOCUS ON
SHARKS

Write your answers on a separate piece of paper.

1. Write a sentence that describes the key ideas in Chapter 2.

2. Do you think countries should continue to allow shark tourism? Why or why not?

3. Which human activity leads to more than 100 million shark deaths each year?

    A. polluting ocean waters
    B. building along coastlines
    C. overfishing

4. Why has the Chinese government stopped serving shark fin soup at events?

    A. The soup is too expensive for most people.
    B. Too many sharks are killed to make the soup.
    C. People do not like the soup's taste anymore.

Answer key on page 32.

GLOSSARY

bacteria
Single-celled living things. They can be useful or harmful.

conservation
The careful protection of plants, animals, and natural resources so they are not lost or wasted.

ecosystems
The collections of living things in different natural areas.

food chains
The feeding relationships among different living things.

overfishing
The act of catching so many fish that the fish population begins to die out.

predators
Animals that hunt other animals for food.

prey
An animal that is hunted and eaten by a different animal.

sanctuaries
Safe, protected places.

species
Groups of animals or plants that are similar.

tourism
When people visit an area for recreation.

TO LEARN MORE

BOOKS

Skerry, Brian. *The Ultimate Book of Sharks*. Washington, DC: National Geographic Children's Books, 2018.

Stein, Lori. *Sharks!* New York: Liberty Street, 2016.

Woodward, John. *Ocean: A Visual Encyclopedia*. New York: DK Publishing, 2015.

NOTE TO EDUCATORS

Visit **www.focusreaders.com** to find lesson plans, activities, links, and other resources related to this title.

INDEX

Australia, 14, 27

China, 19, 26
conservation, 25, 29

ecosystem, 6–7, 12

finning, 18, 26
food chain, 6–8

overfishing, 17–18

predator, 5–6
prey, 5–6, 8–9, 14

sanctuaries, 26–27
seagrass, 12–15
shark fin soup, 19, 26, 28

species, 6, 8–9, 12, 14, 17, 26

tourism, 22–23

United Nations, 26